CW00502680

F-ING
the
SYSTEM
poems by Kayla Henry

FIRST EDITION: 2023
This edition first published in 2023

ISBN 978-1-7777662-6-9 (paperback edition)

Kayla Henry

www.kaylahenryonline.com

To the poets of pen

and poets of heart

and to my grandfather who always taught me to
"be the hammer, not the nail."

CONTENTS

FOREWORD

During the past few years, I have been experiencing the world through a new lens. Though at times it seems like I'm the only one wearing the glasses, I still find a sense of peace in this perceived solitude— I say "perceived" because the more I observe the more I realize that I am not so alone on this path. In fact, I am more connected to a greater number of people and to myself than ever before.

In the past I was quite introverted, but I see now that this was just the result of a long history of surface level connections that left me uninspired. Within my circles we would discuss our common interests and the things we agreed upon, pepper in a bit of gossip, and that was a relationship. Buried in this toxic pattern I could not see why these interactions felt so empty. Now I know. I don't want to talk about the weather, the most popular television series right now, or celebrity drama. I don't want to frolic in echo chambers or agree to disagree. I want to get to the bottom of things, explore the uncomfortable. I want to tiptoe into the improbable, and, above all, I want to create art that reflects that journey.

I hope these poems spark your consciousness, hum, and buzz in your psyche, and offer you the inspiration you may need to find yourself.

Poetry has become such a wonderful outlet. It allows me to get to know myself and my surroundings. Whether I'm fired by an interesting word or rhyme, or the exploration of a new concept, poetry acts as the digestive period in the conceptualization of my worldview. I would say that my pen is driven by a need to wrap my head around my experience here on Earth. Each poem in this collection reflects the reality of the moment in which I wrote it. All I ask from you, as the reader, is that you do not try to figure out my intentions behind each poem; I would much rather you view them through your own lens and see where that takes you.

Thank you for reading.

F-ING
the
SYSTEM

poems by Kayla Henry

STATUS QUO

ENSEMBLE

We're all separated,
preaching to our choirs.
But should we not aim
just a little bit higher?
We rage about inflation,
racism, intimidation,
mistreatment of the elderly,
children, first nations,
police brutality,
what we do with our bodies,
how we choose to raise families,
and even who suffers from more inequalities.
Yet we shy away from personal responsibility
and let "higher-ups" dictate our stories,
　　　　　our value.
Putting us all in the same box
or in different ones when it suits.
Isn't life more fulfilling
when we wear our own shoes?
If some win a war
the others surely lose,
so why would we be at war
with nothing to gain?
Why do we fight over every aspect
of our lives?
It's time we realize
that when we all try to fit
under one small umbrella
we leave no room to dance—
this cannot be our agenda.

We're desperately trying to navigate
rules and ideals
we did not create.
We couldn't see the real issue
if it slapped us in the face:
formed to function to fulfill
another's fate.
Break the mold; reform
into one's true shape.
Pointing fingers at each other,
we only leave room for hate.
When we ignore the problems
we create with every solution
we worsen our state—
allowing more friction.
How can we move past
this cycle of contradiction
when so focused on trivial alliances,
nitpicking at someone's life choices,
drowning out reality with such petty noises?

Walk away and never consent
to the misuse of our voices.
They're meant to connect us,
bring understanding and inspire
not stoke the already flaming
ideological fire.
Can you truly be right
whilst getting pleasure
from someone else being wrong?
Why are we fighting
when we need to get along?

I know it sounds cheesy,
but can we not all agree
that we all grieve
           for something?

For the dying, the poor,
for this class war
           that's rising?
There's one simple moral:
           NO stealing.
That goes for life, health, freedom
and someone's hard earnings.
If we move in this direction
we'll see a new page turning.

History is in the past.
The future is not writ.
And shifting our perspectives
requires no regulations or permits.
We're designed to lose,
confined and restrained.
But when we liberate our minds,
we reclaim our freedom to change.

CONFLICT CATTLE

Putting band-aids on bullet wounds.
Watching them fester
while standing proud:
masquerading good gestures.

To treat us like idiots—
well surely we are
as we've let lousy rhetoric
string us along this far.

I could cry but I won't.
I could scream but I don't
see the point when no one will listen.
Disjointed by words and driven
       by apprehension.

As much as we want
to curse leaders who only gain,
WE sit with empty pockets
and ventriloquized brains.

Do we thrive bound to language
we were never taught to read,
or do we live better lives
when we plant our own seeds?

AMNESTY

No.
It's not enough
to recognize failure.
Forgiveness for the self
and others
comes after effort
is made to amend.
Once cause is acknowledged,
so the same
cannot happen again.

RAT RACE

Biggest bread and circus
in the palm of your hand.
Drawing focus,
videos and brands
fuel the endless cycle
of buy, rinse, repeat.
Again, we are crippled.
Cry from defeat.
Credit debt, loans,
needing that cheat
       code.
'Cause we're all stuck
on this rollercoaster ride.
Our final destination
is unmerited pride.
We've accomplished nothing
and purchased it all.
On the rat race to riches
we sweat 'til we fall.

PARTICIPATION MEDAL

If everybody wins,
then we're all losers.
Simultaneous beggars and choosers.
Create conflict elsewhere.
Healthy competition is rare.
So now we'll pick sides.
No more games, just
divides.

SUPER

Heroes make us passive;
we're waiting on a miracle,
something grand to happen.
Signing off our burdens
to the lone warrior.

When will we learn
to be our own saviors?

WOKE CROWD

We are the conditioned,
seeing offense in ordered letters.
We misinterpret to divide.
Unaware with ruffled feathers.
We will hide behind words:
such feeble battle shields.
Lack motive for revolution
when alone at the wheel.

JUST THE SURFACE

Managing insecurities
with plastic. Surgeries
don't help a broken mind.
New faults to obsess over
in even less time.

SELF-PARALYZING

What existence can be savored
when utterly deprived
of empowerment through challenges?
Numb but still so scared to die.
Make no peace with certain suffering.
Existing in this poison lie.
Keen on scheduled infusions,
completely normalized.
Performing diagnosis,
addictions come justified.
Hooked on chemical replacement—
a surrogate for precious life.

DEVOLUTION

Step down from the vanity
of being "evolved."
Our species still
has much left to solve.
We scoff at ancient Greeks,
seeing Gods in the clouds,
while our sense of belonging's
found in uniform crowds.
Feeling so God-like
connected by phones;
our progress has led us
to being alone.

THE CURTAIN

CAVERNS

They'd been playing in the shadows
for far too long.
So sunken in comfort,
the sun no longer shone.

THE UNTOUCHABLES

What would you do
if you met your idol?

Would you cry and scream,
while they crossed the street,
with the hoard of other NPCs?

Will you amount to anything
if you only chase dreams
of success based on status
or time on-screen?

Appreciate art
but don't reduce yourself
to a background actor
for someone else.

As you obsess over drama
that holds your attention,
your famished mind
falls too weak for objection.

Will you be a creator
or become the lessor
to the ego you spoil
with subconscious depressors?

Wasting imagination
on tantalizing fiction;
it's time you give rest
to this icon addiction.

And then you will step
into the greatest unknown,
once seemingly untouchable
as it was not your own.

MAGIC

Unattainable, unimaginable.
So far out of human control,
yet we accept it on the daily
without any recall.

Whether wizards in capes
or judges in robes,
we fabricate authority
with titles sewn in clothes.

Leaders sworn in by tradition.
Hand on heart and ancient book.
Grandiose buildings, guarded pavilions
filled with actors, thieves, and crooks.

We are dazzled by the rituals,
incantations, speeches, spells.
Bewitched by printed notes of numbers
that wind or rain could render null.

Yet we entertain the make-believe
on payment-plan technologies
and fall oblivious to parallels
in our imposturous reality.

COWARD

If someone takes the reins
they must earn our trust
through truthful discourse
not power lust.

Speak TO the people
before you speak FOR us.

LOOK OVER HERE!

STOP RIGHT NOW!
STOP WHAT YOU'RE DOING!
A STORM IS BREWING
ACROSS THE COUNTRY!
THIS IS NOT JUST A BREEZE.
TAKE COVER A.S.A.P.!

Headlines speak
louder than thought.
Read a little deeper.
It's not
what you think.
If you scan,
if you blink,
you'll miss the real report
and perhaps you'll be hiding
from the wrong thing.

Papers make money
and blogs need a spot,
so read the whole entry
or you might as well not.
Place your critique
between each line.
Contrast and compare
and you'll soon find
you've been lured into traffic
and ads and sick
character defamation
just there for clicks.

Choose your entertainment wisely
'cause sometimes it sinks

in
a little
too deep.

NEWS-SPEAK

Dear Madam News Anchor,
do you sleep at night?
Or are you blind to our rights
and freedoms taking flight?

As you read your prompter,
I can't help but wonder
if you know what you speak
echoes like thunder.

Feeding the beast
that grips our youth,
the only source
they're told is real news.

These mainstream names
are on the path to defame
those who report
without selling us short.

I could curse the 2D faces
behind protective screens
but I'll let it go black
and process what I've seen.

As you do your job
I shall do mine
by studying your claims
and drawing the line

between what has been honest
and what has been funded
by cunning profiteers
and those they've corrupted.

HEADLINE DIET

While humans crave unity,
media fuels division,
leaving no time for criticism.
Falsities – revisions buried
under the next big story.
The damage is done.
And so we go on
as dominoes of irrelevance.
Low context – all tangents.
Worldview through influence.
Who has truly won?

THE TOXIC COMPARE

It could be worse.
We've got it better here.
I'm sick but others are dying,
so in comparison I must be thriving.
My scale for success
relies on others suffering.
So *my* life is peachy
as long as *yours* isn't easy.
I'll wait until
I'm worse off than you
to recognize problems
far overdue.

BABY BIRD

Pre-chewed information
seems easier to swallow.
Do you know where it's been?
Remaining infantile,
you'll take what's given
and passively follow.
Avoid any exertion
to serve this hollow
lifestyle you've chosen:
to lead without course,
as your stomach twists
with no hint of remorse.

REMOTE CONTROL

A pandemic of complacency.
A lack of personal agency.
Programmed to view corruption
as television fantasy.

HYPNOSIS

Tread lightly when consuming today's news.
Cloaks are tailored for everything
                                    even the truth.

CON-VENIENCE

On the shore, a lone sailor
offers you a ride.
And in pause for thought
you recall the times
he harbored few
after boarding many.
Demanded compensation
when halfway at sea.
And now, desperate traveller,
you dare tell me
you'd embark just this once
without pause or worry?

RED FLAGS

Only true fools
are robbed without warning.
Red flags, seldom abrupt,
are raised before waving.

PAPER SHIELDS

Why do you run
from difficult questions?
A lack of answers—
a defense mechanism?
Do you fear uncovering
illogic in your ways?
Are you shaken by change
in your stagnant haze?
How will you learn
without a desire to find,
and with the paper shield
you cower behind?

SET YOUR TABLE

When honesty is conspiracy,
contradiction halts reality,
leads to guts unhealthy
and unequipped for answers.
Preferring childish banter,
we plant the only seeds
we cannot harvest during winter.
Empty plates and minds at dinner
as our consciousness grows thinner.

RUNNING PARADOX

Fear nature.
Fear nature.
Wild things in the wood.
Fear nature.
Fear nature.
Vegetation that could
kill you in an instant
or give you a rash
brushing against skin
while you're walking past.

Yes, run to the concrete.
The buzz and the dust
succumb to bad habits:
excess and lust.
Seek thrills made of plastic
and love built on lies.
Easy access to pills
so your troubles may hide
while you work to pay off
those stale chicken coops
stacked one on the other.
Wishing you could just mute
the noise outside
and the rattle in your head.
But at least around the corner
you're easily fed.
As you complain about farmers
and methane and gas,

you fume in your traffic,
chemically de-weed your grass,
and you lather your skin
with big corp. perfumes,
recline to screen flashes
of DOOM and GLOOM.
Then parade as a citizen,
shout just what you should…

But fear nature.
Fear nature.
It's for your own good...

PERSPECTIVE

ILLUMINATED

Though the outer world may seem
immovable at times,
perspective grants power
to those who remain undefined
by wavering anomalies.
Yes, perspective clarifies
what lies beyond the rubble
and flashing neon signs.

ROLLERCOASTER

In a life lacking balance
the lows weigh tons,
so highs must compare.
And here
births the addiction
to peaks and falls
with one recurring destination.

PACIFY

Singing louder
as the train of horror rolls by.
Singing prouder
to drown out malevolence.

Frozen from action
as you stand with the masses
at the hands of scared men
cradling weapons—

dirt coats your knees.
If only you knew
that by standing in unison
they'll become the few.

The good can't stand tall
without strength in their backs
and evil prevails
while you sing by the tracks—

and so it shall vanquish
if good does not act.

MOUTH TRAP

Fear can be a tranquilizer
or an energizer,

but it is NOT a healthy mind's equalizer.

Fear can bring passivity,
so choose wisely.

A quiet mouth leaves room for assessment:
a great investment,
to think before responding
so you truly understand it.

Do not quell your discoveries.
It would be a tragedy
to walk away silently,
glancing past your shoulder spitefully.

EMOTION

She reminds me of my humanity,
but tends to wander aimlessly.
I hold her tight
as I fear she might
be a misleading friend.

FEEBLE

Be offended
and take that in.
Question why
your skin's so thin.
Have you blocked out reality
to such a degree
that you're whiplashed
by even the slightest debris?

When real trouble comes,
            what then?
Will you grovel about?
Will you mask what's within?
Will you shout your distaste?
            Will the walls just cave in?

To be strong is not wrong.
To take jokes is good character.
Finding harm in clouds—
will you survive harsher weather?

KNOW BETTER

Moral superiority
is not sustainable practice.
If you don't see value in all beings,
does that make you an activist?
If you divide with your pride
so your ego can't fall
then your moral superiority
is not moral at all.

STRAW MEN TELL THEIR TALES

Hours and days.
Weeks and years.
That's how long you barely skim the surface
of one issue or another,
though all have value - all have purpose.

You cannot solve world hunger
while you aim to cure the plague.
But if you stay specific
you may solve *something* one day.

Lack of logic seeps
through unrelated thoughts.
Pray tell, what are you to gain
harping on subjects that they're not?

Hear it first before you burst
with extraneous insistence.
As you're boiling to respond,
you are spawning more resistance.

If you desire your own echo
go and converse with yourself.
But if you seek to know,
listen closely before you tell.

In an attempt to turn the tables,
keep the resolution pure.
Don't harp on comrade's kryptonite—
you'll lose your audience for sure.

And if you're in collusion,
beware the unconditioned.
As an untainted pure reflection
may expose your
                    misdirection.

PERCUSSION

Should we fuel an environment
that perpetuates collisions?

Settling into our comforts,
we lose sight of our visions.

Gain a higher vantage point
by acknowledging your prison.

Feeding petty conflicts
won't favor fruitful action.

BRAWN

After words proven feeble
comes force and fists.
Intellectual battles lost
drives ego to persist.
With no logic left for reason,
live as ignorance were bliss.

DIZZINESS

Stumbling to-and-fro,
increasingly unstable.
Cannot focus in.
What is conscious?
What is fable?
Is opinion self-assembled
or just set on the table?
Thirsty for anything,
       I'll sit
and down the free prosecco.

WHO ARE YOU?

Are you a hero
if the medal 'round your neck is cold?
Are you a hero
if you are doing what you're told?
What defines your greatness
is not in someone else's book.
If you mold yourself to be
the hero in an external story,
the glory will be temporary
and you will fall trying to fit
with the others in the snake pit.

ATLAS

How do we discuss?
How may we comprehend
holding the world on our backs
while barely holding conversation?
Conflict fueled by anticipation.
Only defense is condescension.
Only expense is true connection.
Seeking echoes and reflection.
Watch the quickened denigration,
dispassionate and unenlightened.

EARTHQUAKE

Begin with a thought.
Begin with a question
or a previous certainty
that could use more attention.
When searching for truth
one thing is for certain:
you cannot begin
boasting blind conclusions

lest we quake on our foundation
of unfounded opinions.

IN-FORM

Information,
though often mistaken
for knowledge,
is a series of words,
numbers,
observations
for you to consider.
As pieces of puzzles
are not a full picture.
Though one piece fits,
it may belong in another.
Discernment is key—
or stay *in* form forever.

LIMINALITY

In transition,
the status quo
is parallel
with the unknown.

A new world
with pastures green,
while in the threshold,
remains unseen.

Perhaps this new world
is painted gold
to take you further
from self-control.

A frightening place:
the precarious middle.
You become so restless,
all outs seem desirable.

Recognize change.
Remain wise in the liminal.

THE GREAT EXPLORER

The great explorer travelled
through space and time.
Never flew through sky,
never neared the tracks,
but opened a book,
sought out the wise.
He soaked in the world—
the current and past.
This great explorer
with perception so vast
still walks upon his virgin feet.

LIGHTHOUSE

Values are immovable pillars
through daily gentle whispers
and in titanic roaring thunder.
There to combat paradox.

Stabilizer when suddenly shaken,
reminder when mistaken,
a consistent voice of reason
through even abrupt shocks.

Never bend to the situation,
or mold to convenient opinion.
They force one to awaken
when tempted by the flock.

CONNECTION

ATTRACTION

Do you know what you want?
Hell-bent on expectations,
judging characters outside,
burying *your* afflictions deep.

Magnetic to the aimless
as you share the same conditions.
If you are what you attract,
your betterment remains unwritten.
Will you advance or linger with
other self-prophetic victims?

MISSED CONNECTIONS

Stop fearing loneliness.
You will walk past all the right people
marching hand-in-hand with placeholders.

THE RIGHT FIT

Humans in the pursuit of love
draw in what they're ready for.
The pool is congested
with temporary entertainment.
If claiming to deserve better,
consider personal refinement.

UNBALANCED

Discourteous men
and bitter women:
a noxious by-product
of a mindset broken.

"EMPOWERED"

Your beauty is a commodity.
Your waist is to be wasted.
Empowered by exposition.
Yes, the pigs are elated.

DIVINE PAIR

What has become of the pair?

The undeniable energy
of a closer balance.
Now we war for dominance.
We are made with divine difference,
but we stare enviously
and deny our sharing
of the greatest gift bestowed
upon our ungrateful souls.

We covet abilities
we do not possess
and tear down the opposite
until nothing is left,
with little to show
but our empty breasts.

MY LOVE

I stopped killing flowers when I met you.
It's just the order of things.
I learned to be and to let go.
Found comfort in the unknown
and solace by your bedside.
And in your eyes I saw myself
            happier than ever.
In a focus shift I saw the twinkle
            that you knew.
And in the pause: a frozen world.
            Just me and you.

HER

Beautiful and capable
not neutralized
by shifted labels,
not fetishized
or defined by sexuality.
Not a preference
but a calling, yes.
To be a creator—
a mother of nature.
She will embrace
the pains that try her
with love so pure
she will endure
with grateful light.
She is much more
than just the physical.
She is Woman.
She is inimitable.

MASCULINE

He stood tall,
regarding the horizon
showered in opportunity.
Backbone driven,
mind on men
who ventured before him.

TO CREATE OR TO WAIT

Every few years
a new collapse looms.
We freeze in fear,
tiptoeing through
the major event
that was said to consume us.

And in that time
we scramble for the key
to a threat without reason.
But even in times
of great distress
only those who had skin
in the game were left.
The need to carry on
is fueled by great purpose.
With reason we rise,
but in fear remain aimless.

COMMUNITY

Surround yourself with energy
that pushes you to be better.
Cherish the honest speakers,
the careful listeners,
but beware the comfort choirs
and paper-thin enablers.

ASCH

Self doubt is the catalyst
for conformity.
When the crowd
dictates your identity
because you tremble
at the thought of

                    thinking,

instead, you spend your life

                    hoping

that everyone you were

                    following

had it all figured out.
But that doubt
will eat away at you.
Only fools
put their lives
into the hands of those
who are thinking
that way too.

Dancing in a conga line
with no direction,
circling the drain
without progression.

I WISH YOU COULD SEE

I wish you could see
the smiling faces.
I wish you could hear
the affirmations
of love and unity,
resonating community,
grounded in the earth,
magnetized by the energy
of families
leading themselves to victory.
The only signal we need
is love.

For ourselves,
for the children,
observe the many generations
saying: "never again."
This too shall end
through the power of a pen.
This is a call to action through reaction
as we echo through the nation.
The waves crossing oceans:
freedom in motion.
With an undeniable vibration,
we breathe again
knowing we can.
We laugh, we dance.

I wish you could see.

INNOCENCE

RENEW

I was born screaming—
not out of fear
but to express
my newfound presence.
I was born with wonder
as my hands could wander
on every novel surface.
I laughed in joy of new experience,
inspired in my existence
but vulnerable in my innocence.
Having so much to assert,
yet to find the words,
I looked to my mother
who gave me a voice for this world.

The moment I was ready
to reveal my truest self
I was put through a new story
that was not mine to tell.
My WHYs were often met
with a rigid BECAUSE.
I lost feeling in my lips,
no longer mine to move.
Wistful was the disposition.
I had not understood
why my eagerness for answers
was not proper — was not good.
And here I sit years later
searching for that wonder
I lost somewhere between.
I can see the faintest glimmer.

A SIMPLE REMINDER

Born beautiful,
this you must know.
Eroded by all
who wish you weren't so.

CHILD-ISH

How silly we were
as children.
We were wild,
playing dragons.
"I'm a cat!" "I'm a dog!"
Could you imagine
a world where we never
grew up?
Born human
but never guided:
perpetual pups.
Make-believe forever,
fantasy-struck.

SECONDHAND

I have cried for the children
abused in their innocence,
inhaling the smoke
of their parents.
Thwarted vicariously
through the self-indulgence
and in the fear
of generations too scared
to know themselves.

FOR THE FUTURE

It starts with children.
Don't let them become
the scared men and women
we are today:
driven by stories,
falling in line.
Though similar story tellers
have fooled us time
and time again.

How can we fend
for ourselves
when we eat
the poison they sell,
with a shovel
adorned with excuses?
Accustomed to the abuses
and our attitude is:
no time, not enough money.
Don't want to lose this
life we're living
of monotonous 9 to 5-ing,
busied by addictive distracting,
no reflection of the self.
Convinced we're thriving
thinking health
is found by prescribing.

We're just relying
on everyone but ourselves,
leaving no chance to develop

our own generational wealth.
But that's not weighed in money.
It's measured in values
and skills passed on
that will carry us through
no matter the political climate,
the price of food,
no matter the new fear
or victim trend.

The message we send
when we subscribe
and pretend
that normal means
whatever you feel each morning
is the immovable reality of the day.
And those who say
otherwise are insensitive.
Enabling is easier.
Self-knowledge is too much effort.
Self-healing is not mainstream.
Yet in hospitals and care homes
we wait to be seen,
but it seems
we are forgotten.
Better fed in some prisons.

In nature we must listen.
Remember what we've been given
here on earth
before the other distractions:
the big corporations,

fabricated societal expectations,
flip-flop-for-votes politicians.
Because no matter how
you twist your vision,
humans need food and water.
We have no existence
without mothers and fathers.
Nature has patterns:
spring, summer, fall, winter.
Perspectives are gained
in past and present for future.
But the only thing you can *change*
is what you do with the now.
So let children live slowly.
It seems *we've* forgotten how.

THE FIELD

We cannot all fit
into this monochrome picture.
Instead of feeding strengths,
we punish the future
of the children gifted
outside set curriculums.
Made to feel dumb
but they're not the only ones
struggling to pay attention.

Yet they're sent to detention
as they aren't stimulated
by this weird simulation—
a twisted reality
where all must be equally
                treated
until they haven't succeeded,
then they're shamed.
They're defeated
by those who misled them
                in the first place.

We all work at our own pace.
These kids burning to escape—
it's right in your face:
they don't fit the shape
they're being carved into.

They're not like you.

They see past those walls.

94

They won't march
like ants down the hall
when the lunch bell calls.
Their spirits run through fields
past the bricks that shield
from the outside world.

What have we prepared them for?
When they leave through those doors
they are anxious and unsure
of how finances work,
how law language is obscured,
and scared that purpose is defined
by a piece of paper they procured,
                          or did *not* procure.

That's not the point of existence.
Why is it that the different
are met with such resistance?
We should encourage their persistence
to question the systems.

Why follow the same crowded path?
How many roads are on a map?
And who are you to hold back
the ones
          who run
                    through the field
                                        instead?

BEAUTIFUL RISKS

Where are the children
in the dirt and mud
with cuts and bruises?
The careful explorers?
The unbiased detectives?
The open hearts
with fresh perspectives?
Imperviously playful,
free from directives?
Those set to breach
homogeneous collectives?

ODE TO CHILDHOOD

She was a brave girl—
conjuring swords from sticks,
leaping from mountain-hills,
demanding answers
and imagining possibilities.

Who are the tyrants
who rob such creatures
of fullness in sincerity?

TANGIBLE

A child watches,
listens,
learns
from the stimulus around him.
So fantastic to observe.
But this twinkle of life
reproduced in LEDs
will never compare
to the tangible reality
that once inspired great minds.

HERE AND NOW

NORMAL-SEA

The fish are tracing circles;
easy targets
bound by habit—
nature's cruelest pattern.
Unaware of their place on this planet.
Remember not their kin
who perished in the same forfeit.

REVOLVING DOOR

To evolve
or to repeat
      repeat
      repeat.
To encounter opportunity
allowing it to change you
or to continue
in circular motion
and repeat
      repeat
      repeat.

POISON EARTH

You are what you eat.
You think what you consume.
No water, no soil;
how will a flower bloom?

WITH THE BUTTERFLY

Why must we give name to all we touch,
cutting it, then, into a thousand pieces?
Dissection grants empowerment?
Lest the unknown may plague us?
Nature has patterns without assistance.
Why must we control? Can we not admire
from a distance?

> Life shifts as needed.
> Grass we have weeded
> still rebels with innate purpose.
> Leave the empty conquest.
> Live harmoniously.
> Some mysteries
> are best left as they are;
> beautifully unaltered
> by selfish curiosity.

AIR

Come play again.
Run through the forest with me.
Let your fingertips trace the leaves.
Begin again,
breathing free.

PEPPER

A creator lives,
breathes,
steps away from
the drawing board
to live.
And that life
is seasoned
—spiced
with rich aromas.

Stop fabricating.
Begin listening.
Begin living.
Creation will come
when you become
alive.

A METAPHOR

We are beauty
on the precipice of bloom.
And yet we sit
in pots on concrete,
masking faults
we constantly prune.
And in our cells
we're silenced.
Seeds could never sound
until realizing soil
comes freely from the ground.

IN TIME

DIS-EASE

Biohacking natural course,
as if we are above it.
So much so that we lose
ourselves in the process.
Stunting our ability
to evolve naturally,
we devolve spiritually.
Removing ourselves
from understanding the beauty
of life and death.

So we live in fear of it.
Trying to change it.
And even sometimes
ostracizing those
          who just let it be—
those who trust the biology
that's gotten us so far.

Is it healthy
to have no faith
in your own body?
If you're convinced you can't
take care of yourself,
where do you go?:
To the abusers who know
you're impaired
by lack of direction.
Predators need victims.
Symptoms
are your body adapting

and wisdom
is letting it happen.

Will you desperately
run to a pharmacy
to ease temporarily
without allowing yourself
to overcome instinctively?
If we numb these battles
we reject the opportunity
to realize our strength
is not outwardly granted;
       it's innate.
We cause our victimhood
when we never create
       and only consume.

Embrace a helpless mentality,
or the solutions built in you?

SLOW DOWN

Running for the sake of running.
If I stop, I risk confronting
heavy shadows strung along.
The quickened pace: evasive song.
I mustn't leave.
I may soon see.
And when I do, I'll bask in light
I could not catch in aimless flight.

I WANT

How long has it been since you smoked
a cigarette?
How long has it been since you drank
yourself sick?
How long has it been since a big tv binge?
How often do you eat a last-minute fast fix?
Are you burdened by what is not in your
control?
Fill temporary desires
or nurture your soul?

RUT

Oh, the drifters—
Crowd-induced
shape shifters.
Each passing day
leaves minute fissures.
Until the dusk
where they stay wake,
deeply troubled.
Voices ache
knowing hours
have more to offer.
Stirred by regret
'til morning after.

PRODUCTIVITY

The clock, engorged
with your excuses,
soon strikes twelve.
Yet you've found no solutions
and you listen
as the seconds

tick on

tick on

Now that actionable moment
is wasted.

Gone.

How many revolutions
will you sit upon
until you tire of droning
and get something done?

DETACHED

We grieve at our loss of appetite for action
as we huddle with the masses
waiting impatiently for purpose
to save us from the chill
of worthlessness.

Though it may be hard to hear:

She who looks to another
to bestow her with intention
will never be the mother
of her own invention.

TICKING AWAY

And so we wait
we wait
we wait
upon the fevered to stand.
And so we wait
we wait
we wait
for inspiration from the void.
And so we wait
we wait
we wait
unable to pretend
we are worthy of something great.
And so we wait
we wait
we wait
again
and again.

BIGGER PICTURE

I am no accident.
My blood travels.
My lungs fill, somehow,
without my instruction.
And yet
I am ill content
with the environment
around me.
The conflicts surrounding
are one with my being.
If this weren't so,
why would I be here?

Why do I rise with the sun?
Why do trees
mimic my lungs
without ever meeting—
never learning
to function together?
The sky brings weather
that keeps me fed,
and yet
I still wonder
why I'm here...

I was created in harmony
with all around me.
I am not just an entity.
I am a lifeform in a much greater body.

RELIGIOSITY

My body: my church.
My mind: a steeple.
Oh, the peaceful within
requires no rehearsal.
Though powers shift
and institutions crumble,
through space and time
stands the inner temple.

LIGHT

And though our ears
may no longer hear
the affirmations,
you are born again
through smiles and tears
shed by those who reminisce.
We will be guided.
You will be blessed
as love is eternal.

The lessons traced
in the sand displaced
by your purposed footsteps
will bring us comfort
as we step into the unknown.
You are by our side,
in our minds.

Let us renew
as we pass through
this changing tide
together.
Let us be wise
as we take on
the wondrous world
you leave behind
in stride.

Release your shoulders.
Our strength will grow from memory
and your wisdom bestowed.

Between the fall and rise
of sky, blue-pink,
we will rest with you
and recount the many times
you crossed our minds
and you will have peace.

Your voice now an echo;
your spirit a beacon.
All you believed shall be
as anything is possible in dream
and within your bright legacy.

Sleep now.
Embrace those
you've missed for so long.
We make beauteous this world
while on earth
and after gone.
And so you have
and so you will.

AGAINST THE GRAIN

PARALLEL

The paths are made quite clear.
They will not meet.   They will not veer.
In the middle humans wander,
chasing
lines
drawn
by
a
stranger.

THE UPSIDE IS DOWN

I hurt for the hearts of this world
drowning in misery
shaded from beauty.
With word-soups and labyrinths,
fearing lives lived peacefully.

HUSH

The more we censor what we say
the less in tune with our thoughts we become.

If we can consciously tape our own mouths
how is it we can trust ourselves?

No longer will we think openly
if we have shunned our minds,
caged our consciousness
from knocking at the walls evermore.

Neither seen nor heard.
Like a child deemed
too difficult to raise
so chosen to be ignored.

LISTEN

A scream will echo
for all to hear,
but a whisper
rewards the listeners
who wait for secrets,
while the preoccupied
soak in cries
of little significance.

IN ALL CIRCUMSTANCES

What does it mean to have bodily autonomy?
Freedom of choice does not end with a policy.
Moral dilemmas are an individual battle.
We are human beings—
do not rob us our paddles.
Take our money, our time—
make life a hassle.
But my body is MINE.
Do not govern my temple.

FINE PRINT

Diversions.
Diversions
lead us astray,
burden our minds,
tax our days
while blind lead blind.
Shouting 'til we drown ourselves—
no thoughtful pause to turn around
and walk the other way.
We say we're fighting for the greater good,
yet our hours waste on cardboard signs
and in online time—
attempting to remind
everyone we have a voice
while we disappear within the noise.

Have we forgotten
we have a choice in the matter?
Must we participate
in the "I know better" race,
or can we turn the other way?
Where minutia doesn't shatter us,
and big collapse can't burden us
'cause simplicity is the focus.
Paying into what we complain about,
we stoke every fire the more we shout.
Lining up at the trough
for our new identity:
homogeneous individuality.
Pigs on the farm
become what they are.

We succumb to the very thing
we claim to oppose.
Why play within this game?
A game made to overcomplicate
the basics of life.
Lift the curtain
to see the roaches
we know are there?
Spare the trouble and just stop feeding them.
Feed yourself.
Leave hate under the rubble,
leave fear-traps alone;
they're trouble.
And you'll be free
to be,
to live
harmoniously
with the ground below your feet.

There's no need to compete
for a prize that's fleeting.
A prize that relies
on values compromised
for the sake of comforts
granted by the very same
who can snatch them back
in an instant.
Using justifications
designed to favor the system
in which you willingly participate.
You'll continue diving into matters
that only exist to consume you

and forget the truth:
there is no fine print in freedom.

THE PLACE

I wished for an earth that nobody wanted
where we lived by our brows
and confronted our fears
with awareness of the temporary
and distrust in the arbitrary—
where our goals did not sleep
under anthills and sweets
and upward we trekked
without rotting our teeth.
I wished for an earth
it seemed nobody wanted...

HOLLOW

I was in a dream
listening to banter.
Empty laughs about the weather.
Became an alien observer
in a conversation lacking substance.

Will I get used to this?

OBSOLETE

Daily dissonance
over lifelong fulfillment.
The choice is made
when you stay snug.
Apathy is a calling
swept under the rug.

MASCOT

I will not play this role.
Eggshells 'round the verbal.
Avoidance of the actual.
This cannot take a toll
on who I could become.
I will be dead and gone
'fore I see the light of dawn.
Oh, please let me move on.
I've grown tired of this run.

OPEN

I don't believe in luck
but I do see synchronicities.
When you take control of your fate
and are open to opportunity
the pieces fall into place—
welcomed by mind and body.

I AM. I WILL.

The battles I wage are my own.
And I will fight them
because I must live.

The hardships I face are mine to bare
and won't be erased by any other;
so I must live.

Time will bend me.
Forces may steer my eyes.
But in wake of change,
I choose to rise,
because I am alive.

I know I am.

FORGIVENESS

Leave behind bitterness.
It will become you.
From the inside out
consume you,
if it's allowed.
You will align
with a crooked life
and find
nothing but mud
in what could be
a valley of flowers.

ANEW

These times may be dark.
These times may burn us.
But we will thrive
within this darkness.
From such paralysis
comes metamorphosis.
With wings on fire
we begin to resurface.

WHAT NOW?

Be you—
the most authentic,
unapologetic, enigmatic,
impervious to static
you.
Your inner fabric
is the baseline
to the solution.
Turn to real value.
Leave behind the valueless
and you'll live without the stress
of pressing through the grinder
of the mundane and meaningless.
Get on with the rest
of what makes life beautiful,
as we are capable
on our own.

MANIFEST

Carry on
your intuition
through stranger times
and situations
that treat you oddly
and whisper softly:
"something is amiss."

Do not wish
in ideal fictions
as wishes stumble
in real motion.
Dreams are faulty.
Conscience guilty
of undeserved gifts.

You are the mover
on your feet,
the frame that holds
the canvas sheet,
and as the painter
bring the colors;
a story only
YOU complete.

And so you will.

ACKNOWLEDGEMENTS

*Thanks to Bria and Vincent
for your help and inspiration.*

Ingram Content Group UK Ltd.
Milton Keynes UK
UKHW011052020623
422771UK00004B/127